Basics

half-hitch knot

Figure 1: Come out a bead and form a loop perpendicular to the thread between beads. Bring the needle under the thread away from the loop. Then go back over the thread and through the loop. Pull gently so the knot doesn't tighten prematurely.

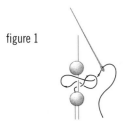

figure 1

crimping

It's a good idea to place a bead between the crimp and the clasp to ease strain on the wire at the crimp. Make sure you can thread the wire through this bead twice.

To crimp with chainnose pliers, simply mash the crimp as flat as possible, making sure the wires aren't crossed inside it. Crimping with crimping pliers involves two steps:

Figure 2: On one end of a length of flexible beading wire, thread a crimp bead then a large-holed bead. Go through one end of the clasp. Bring the wire back through the bead and crimp. Slide the bead and crimp close to the clasp, leaving a small space. Mash the crimp firmly in the hole closest to the handle, which looks like a half moon. Hold the wires apart so one piece is on each side of the deep dent.

Figure 3: Put the dented crimp in the pliers' front hole on end and press hard. This rolls the crimp into a cylinder.

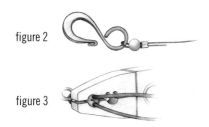

figure 2

figure 3

opening and closing loops

Figure 4: To open a loop or ring, use one or two pairs of pliers to grasp the wire at the opening. Pull one pliers toward you and push the other away to bring the ends of the wire apart and out of the plane of the loop. Never spread the loop side to side, which will fatigue the metal. Close the loop by pulling the ends back into the plane.

figure 4

plain loops

Figure 5: Cut a head or eye pin, leaving a ⅜-in. (1cm) tail above the bead. Bend it against the bead at a right angle with the tip of a chainnose pliers.

Figure 6: Grip the very tip of the wire in roundnose pliers. If you can feel it when you brush your finger along the back of the pliers, the loop will be teardrop-shaped.

Figure 7: Press the pliers downward slightly to avoid pulling, and rotate the wire into a loop. Let go, regrasp the loop at the same place on the pliers, and keep turning to close the loop. The closer to the pliers' tip that you work, the smaller the loop.

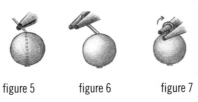

figure 5   figure 6   figure 7

wrapped loops

Figure 8: Leaving a 1-in. (2.5cm) tail, place the tip of a chainnose pliers against where the bead will be. Bend the tail to form a right angle.

Figure 9: With roundnose pliers, grasp the tail just past the bend and pull it over the jaw to point the other way.

Figure 10: Loosen the pliers grip enough to rotate them so the empty jaw is above the partial loop and continue pulling

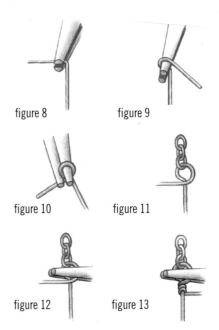

figure 8   figure 9

figure 10   figure 11

figure 12   figure 13

the tail around the bottom jaw until it's perpendicular to the wire.

Figure 11: Pull a split ring, chain, etc., into the loop.

Figure 12: To keep the loop round, grasp it with roundnose pliers in your non-dominant hand above the cross. You can wrap the pliers' jaws with masking tape to avoid denting the wire.

Figure 13: Grasp the tail with chainnose pliers or your fingers to pull it around the wire until it meets the bead. Make the first wrap against the pliers; keep wraps close together. One wrap is sufficient to keep the loop from opening; additional wraps are decorative. Clip. Use chainnose pliers to press in the cut end.

making head pins

Figure 14: Make a tiny U-shaped loop at the end of the wire with the tip of a roundnose pliers, pinch it closed with chainnose pliers, and trim the wire end just above the bend if needed.

figure 14

Make your own chain

M aking your own chain with wire is fun. Add a few beads and a clasp for a stunning necklace and bracelet set. Practice with copper wire, and you'll soon find yourself experimenting with all types of wire and pattern variations.

wire savvy

Wire comes in different gauges, or thicknesses; the higher the number, the thinner the wire. For example: 16-gauge wire is substantial, and 24-gauge is thin.

It's also available in three stiffnesses, dead soft, half hard, and full hard. Some wires are naturally harder that others. Sterling silver is harder than gold-filled, which is harder than copper. In addition, the more wire is hammered or bent, the harder it becomes.

When working with wire, you need to use a flush wire cutter. The flat, or flush, side of the cutter leaves the wire end flat; the beveled side produces a pointed cut. Get in the habit of always starting with a flush cut by snipping off the very tip of your wire with the flat side of the cutter against the wire length.

To make uniform rings, wrap wire around a dowel. Use different sizes of dowels and various wire gauges to change looks. Generally, the thickness of the wire and the dowel should be proportionate.

The necklace and bracelet at left are comprised of triple split rings linked with twisted jump rings. The necklace features a glass center bead and silver bead caps. Notice how using extra-large twisted jump rings on the bracelet adds a surprising and dramatic effect.

triple split rings

❶ Drill a hole the same diameter as the wire through the end of the dowel. Put one end of the wire through the hole and bend it to secure it to the dowel. Wrap the wire tightly around the dowel at least 114 times to make 38 triple split rings. Wind each revolution straight and right against the previous wrap (**photo a**).

❷ With the cutter flush against the last wrap, cut off the excess wire at both ends and remove the coil from the dowel. Press the cutter lightly between the 3rd and 4th coils even with the cut end to separate the coils (**photo b**) and cut off a triple split ring. Press the coils

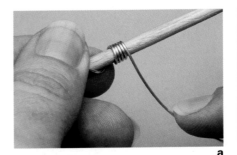
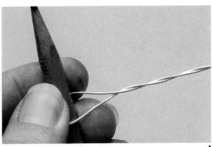

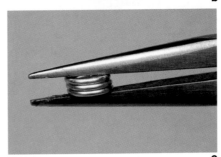

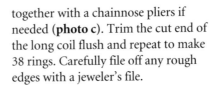

together with a chainnose pliers if needed (**photo c**). Trim the cut end of the long coil flush and repeat to make 38 rings. Carefully file off any rough edges with a jeweler's file.

twisting wire, 2 options

❶ Fold a 2-yd. (1.8m) length of 20-gauge wire in half. Hold the ends with a chainnose pliers or a vise and insert a pencil into the fold.

❷ Turn the pencil (**photo d**) until the twist is tight and even. If it's too tight, it will twist back on itself; if it's too loose, it'll make messy-looking jump rings.

❸ Alternatively, bend the wire in half and insert the ends into the chuck of a hand drill or Coiling Gizmo. Put a pencil in the bend and have a friend hold it. Turn the drill's handle until you achieve the desired twist.

twisted jump rings

❶ Make a 39-ring coil around a dowel with the twisted wire.

❷ Saw the rings off with a jeweler's saw, or snip them as before (**photo e**).

materials, 16-in. (41cm) necklace

- 5½ yd. (5m) 20-gauge Sterling silver wire
- ⅛-in. (3mm) Dowel
- Clasps (or make your own as seen on p. 4)
- 1 Centerpiece bead and 2 bead caps

Tools: round- and chainnose pliers, flush wire cutter, pencil, drill and bit to match wire's diameter, jeweler's file; optional: jeweler's saw with #2 blades, hand drill

putting the pieces together

❶ To make the necklace chain, open the jump rings (see "Basics," p. 3) and string split rings between them (**photo f**). Start and end with a jump ring to which you attach the clasp. For the bracelet, string two small and one large jump ring with a split ring between each.

❷ When you reach the center of the necklace, string your center bead and bead caps on a 6-in. (15cm) length of wire with triple-wrapped loops on each end (see "Basics") and attach this centerpiece to the chain with twisted jump rings. Continue linking the other half of the chain. ❍ – *Lisa Niven Kelly*

Multi-strand necklace

Stretching a small quantity of expensive beads without looking as though you're scrimping isn't always easy. Here's one solution: First, combine a strand or two of expensive beads with inexpensive pearls and a few dozen Swarovski crystals. Second, make lots of strands, stretching the beads by stringing them between lengths of chain on wrapped loops. Third, add quality by using good findings.

To create visual interest, choose beads of different shapes, lusters, finishes, and sizes. Here, the hard sparkle of faceted crystal contrasts with the deep luster of pearls. I've used elongated and round pearls and round and square crystals, and I've added just a few iridescent green crystals to counteract a tendency for the necklace to become too monochromatic.

For a successful random necklace, careful planning is critical. After determining the length of the necklace (mine is 18 in./46cm) and the number of strands (nine), lay out several strands at a time on a jewelry design board. Space the beads irregularly and vary the sizes, kinds, and colors within each strand and across the width of strands.

❶ Attach a split ring to each loop on the clasp.
❷ Subtract the width of the clasp plus split rings from the total length of the necklace. I made the top group of strands about 18 in. long and increased the other two groups by ½ in. (1.3cm) each. Lay out three strands at a time to the determined length by placing an assortment of beads randomly spaced in the grooves of the design board. Spaces between beads will be filled with wrapped loops that connect varied lengths of chain. Remember to allow about ½ in. for the wrapped loops on each bead.
❸ Cut a piece of wire for each bead 2 in. (5cm) longer than the bead to allow for small wrapped loops. Begin a wrapped loop an inch from one end of a wire piece and thread on the bead. Bend the wire at a right angle about ⅛ in. (3mm) past the bead and begin the other wrapped loop (**photo a**). Do not wrap either loop. Repeat for each bead on the strand.

materials

necklace
- 1 16-in. (41cm) Strand 7.5mm round faceted pearls
- 2 Strands 10mm oblong pearls
- **48** 6mm Round Swarovski crystals
- **18** 6mm Square Swarovski crystals
- 1 3-Strand Gold clasp
- 30-36 ft. (9-11m) 24-gauge Gold-filled wire
- 7-8 ft. (2-2.5m) 2.2mm Gold-filled cable chain
- 6 4.5-5mm Gold-filled split rings

earrings
- 2 Square crystals
- 2 Round crystals
- 2 Faceted pearls
- 4 Head pins
- Earring finding with loop
- 5 in. (13cm) Chain

Tools: Round- and chainnose pliers, diagonal wire cutters; tapestry needle and jewelry design board optional

❹ Start assembling a strand at the center, cutting the chain as you go. Pull one end of the chain into a loop on the center bead and complete the wrap. Place the bead and chain back on the board and cut the chain where it meets the loop on the next bead. Thread the bead onto the chain and complete that wrap (**photo b**). Work outward from the center, connecting chain and bead segments. Check the strand length as you assemble it and make adjustments, perhaps removing beads, as needed.
❺ As you assemble the second and third strands, adjust bead positions as needed. Remember that the more strands you make the fuller the necklace will become, so don't worry if it looks a little skimpy at first.

tip

Wrapped loops

If you haven't made wrapped loops, practice with copper wire or head pins first. – *Alice Korach*

a

b

c

❻ Attach the end of each of the first three strands to the top split rings on the clasp. Attach some strands by connecting the wrapped loop on the last bead to the split ring and attach others by threading the end link of chain onto the split ring (**photo c**).
❼ Unfasten the clasp so you can lay the strands out to plan the next group of three in relation to the first group.
❽ Repeat steps 2-6 for the middle and bottom strand groups.

earring
❶ Begin a very small wrapped loop on each side of the square bead. Thread a 3-link piece of chain onto the top loop and complete that wrap.
❷ String a pearl on one head pin and a round crystal on another and begin a small wrapped loop above each bead. Thread a 13-link piece of chain on the pearl and a 6-link piece on the crystal. Complete the wraps.
❸ Thread the other end of each chain onto the loop below the square crystal and complete the wrap.
❹ If needed, stretch the top link above the crystal with a tapestry needle and thread it onto the loop on the earring finding. Close the loop very tightly.
❺ Make the other earring to match the first. ❍ – *Alice Korach*

Turning wheel earrings

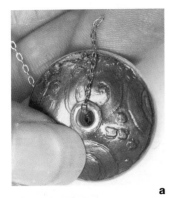

a

c

e

g

b

d

f

materials

- **2** Disk beads with large center holes (copper and silver riveted beads from Chimera Glass Works, chimera@talweb.com)
- 14¾ in. (37.5cm) Sterling silver cable chain, 2.2mm
- 4 in. (10cm) 24-gauge Sterling silver wire, round, half hard
- 6 in. (15cm) 20-gauge Sterling silver wire, round, half hard

Tools: round- and chainnose pliers, diagonal wire cutter, small metal file if making earwires; hammer and anvil or steel block optional

template

Disk- or donut-shaped beads are fun, but making them into earrings can be a challenge. This creative approach uses "spokes" of chain to hang the disks from wire earring findings, evoking bicycle wheels. The disks rotate under the chain and the spokes shift naturally with the movement of the wheels. Their constant movement makes these earrings fun and interesting.

This pair of earrings is made with textured, hollow copper disk beads created by Fae Mellichamp of Chimera Glass Works, but you could use any small disk or donut beads that are light enough to make comfortable earrings.

Wrap the chain through the hole of the bead, join the ends with an unusual version of a wrapped ring, and hang the ring from an earring finding that you make yourself or purchase.

wrapping the bead

❶ Cut the chain into two 7⅜-in.-long (18.7cm) lengths.
❷ Thread one piece through the hole, leaving an end on top that's about ½ in. (1.3cm) longer than the radius of the bead (**photo a**). Then wrap the long end from back to front around the edge and through the hole four times. Keep the wraps next to each other and don't cross the chain over itself as it goes through the hole (**photo b**).
❸ Instead of completing the fifth wrap, bring the end of the chain up to meet the starting end. The chains should end on opposite sides of the disk. Join them with a wrapped ring. Cut a 2-in. (5cm) length of 24-gauge wire and thread it through the last link on each end of the chain. With roundnose pliers, make a fairly large ring in the middle of the wire by crossing the tails around one jaw of the pliers (**photo c**). Slide both chain ends into the loop and jiggle the chain

wraps until the ends are even and the bead hangs straight.
❹ Use chainnose pliers to feed the wire ends through the ring, wrapping it the same way you wrapped the chain around the bead (**photo d**). Make 4-6 wraps as evenly spaced as possible.
❺ When each end of the wire reaches the chain, make a small tight wrap next to the chain on each side of it. Trim the wire tails and press them in with chainnose pliers (**photo e**).

making earwires

❶ If you're using purchased earwires, open the loop on the earring (see "Basics," p. 3) and hang the wrapped ring. Close the loop.
❷ If you're making your own earwires, shape a 3-in. (7.6cm) length of 20-gauge silver wire following the full-size **template** above. Start by making a small spiral for the hanging loop with roundnose pliers (**photo f**). When the spiral matches the template, shape the large

curve with your fingers.
❸ Before wearing the earring, file the end that will go into your ear so it's rounded and smooth. If you wish, hammer both sides of the entire earwire on an anvil or steel block. Then thread the wrapped ring on the wire from the back to the bottom of the spiral (**photo g**).
❹ Make the other earring a mirror image of the first. ❍
– *Alice Korach*

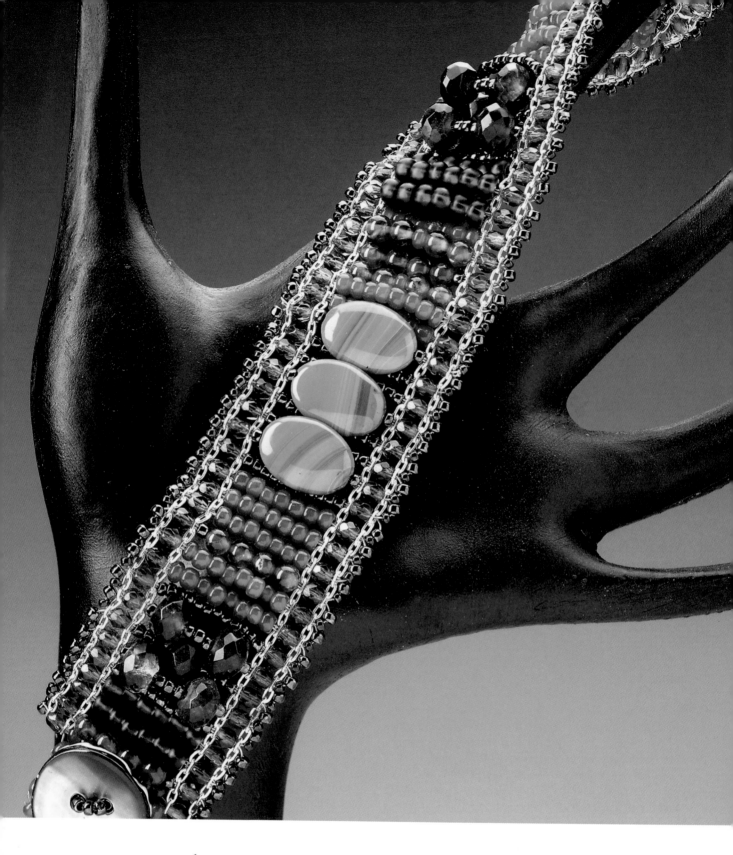

Chained bracelet

This bracelet is based on a European design by a jewelry artist named Ziio. Her bracelet, which appeared in the December 1996 issue of *Bead&Button*, was rather tricky, but this chain version is just as pretty and much easier.

Two long chains form the skeleton of the bracelet and a variety of colorful beads fill out the design. Start the loop end in the middle of both chains. After making the loop, weave the bracelet. End with a button tab.

button loop

❶ Lay both chains on a table with the centers parallel. The top chain will be the "outer" chain, and the bottom one will be the "inner" chain. Identify the center link of each chain.

❷ Cut a 2-yd. (1.8m) length of flexible beading wire. Thread a 15º, an 11º, and a 15º seed bead to the center of the wire. On the outer chain, count 14 links to the left of the center link and pass the wire through that link toward the inner chain. Thread on a 3mm fire-polished (FP) bead and go through the 7th link from the center of the inner chain. Add a 15º seed bead.

❸ With the other end of the wire, skip a link of the outer chain and bring the wire through the 12th link. Thread an FP and go through the 6th link from the center of the inner chain. Bring the first wire through the same (6th) inner link and the FP. The two wires will cross inside the FP. Continue through the same (12th) outer link (**photo a**). You now have one wire exiting each chain.

❹ Thread an 11º and a 15º on the outer wire. Skip a link and go through the 10th. String an FP and go through the next inner chain link (the 5th). Thread a 15º on the other wire, go through the same 5th inner link, the new FP and the same 10th outer link (**photo b**). Repeat this step, skipping one link on the outer chain each time until you have 12 or 13 FPs.

bracelet band

❶ To start the bracelet band, thread an 11º and a 15º on the wire that exits the outer chain. Skip a link and go through the next. String an FP, skip a link on the inner chain, and go through the next.

a

b

c

d

e

f

String enough 8º beads to equal the length of the flat stone bead plus two 11ºs (here 17mm). On the left-hand side of the bracelet, go through the first link below the start on the inner chain. Go through the first FP and the starting outer chain link (**photo c**).

❷ The other wire exits the inner chain on the right-hand side of the button loop. String an 11º and a 15º, go through the link you passed through in step 1, going toward the right. Continue through the FP and the same outer link (**photo d**).

❸ With a wire exiting each side of the bracelet, you are ready to weave the band, crossing the wires in each row of beads. Start each row by stringing an 11º and a 15º on each wire and skipping a link on each chain. String an FP between the chains, then fill in the interior. The interior rows must be the same length as the flat bead plus two 11ºs. The bracelet looks best if you string several rows similarly to form pattern groups.

❹ Work until the band and loop are ½-1 in. (1.3-2.5cm) longer than the circumference of your wrist.

❺ To add wire, center the new piece in the last row. After weaving a few rows, end the old wire by going through the first 2 edge beads and tying a half hitch knot (see "Basics," p. 3 and **photo e**).

materials

- 2 15-in. (38cm) Lengths 2.2mm cable chain
- 1 pkg. Each matching or coordinating seed beads, sizes 6º, 8º, 11º, and 14º or 15º
- 100-120 3mm Fire-polished, faceted beads (FP)
- 3-7 12-15mm-long Flat stone beads
- 10-15 5 x 7mm Contrast-color and shape semi-precious stone beads
- 20-32 4mm Semi-precious stone beads
- 1 ½-⅝-in. (1.3-1.6cm) 2-Hole button
- 6 yd. (5.5m) Flexible beading wire, .010
- #12 Beading needle and Silamide or Nymo D

Tools: wire cutters, chainnose pliers

Pull the knot very tight, go through a few beads in the new row, and clip the tail. Repeat on the other side.

button tab

❶ String an 11º on each wire. Then take each wire back through the same link, FP, and link it exits (**photo f**). Cut off all the excess chain.

❷ Weave 4-6 rows of 8º beads the same width as the interior rows, crossing the wires in each row.

❸ End each wire as in step 5 above.

❹ Use a needle and doubled thread to sew the button on the tab, stringing 2-3 seed beads between the holes on top. ●

– *Sybil Rosen*

Leftover chain elegance

After you've been making jewelry for a while, you'll find yourself with lots of 3-4-in. (7.6-10cm) lengths of leftover chain. They're too good to throw away, but what will you ever do with them? This necklace answers that question beautifully and, in addition, puts to good use some of those leftover beads you've also been accumulating.

Join chain scraps by linking them together with beads and wrapped loops. You can use as many beads as you wish and link them as close or as far apart as the lengths of your chain pieces allow. On this 6-strand necklace, one strand has no beads, but the others have 3-5 beads each.

I used one kind of chain for each strand and only a few beads, but feel free to use different chains in each strand and as many beads as you like. Join the strands that make up the front of the necklace inside cones and use a single chain for the back sections. A clasp and chain closure makes the length adjustable.

If you still have chain left after making the necklace, why not make a bracelet or multi-dangle earrings, too?

❶ Begin by making a beaded segment that will link two pieces of chain. Cut a piece of wire 2-3 in. (5-7.6cm) longer than the bead(s). Start a wrapped loop (see "Basics," p. 3) about 1½ in. (3.8cm) from one end of the wire but don't wrap the loop. Pull the end link of a piece of chain into the loop, then finish the wrap. String the bead(s) on the wire and begin another wrapped loop. Before wrapping, pull the end of another chain piece into the loop (**photo a**).

❷ Assemble six strands of chain and beads as described in step 1. Each strand should be about 10 in. (25cm) long, plus or minus ¼ in. (6mm) and should begin and end with chain.

❸ With a 4-in. (10cm) length of wire, begin a large wrapped loop that will fit inside a cone. Before wrapping, pull one end of each chain strand into the loop (**photo b**).

❹ Thread the wire through the cone, pulling the loop up inside so the ends of the chain are hidden. Then string a 4mm bead or crystal on the wire. Begin a medium-sized wrapped loop and pull a 2-3-in. length of chain into the loop before wrapping (**photo c**). Repeat steps 3-4 on the other end of the necklace.

❺ For the hook end of the clasp, start a wrapped loop on a 2-3-in. length of wire and attach it to the end of one of the back chains before wrapping. String a 4mm bead on the wire and begin another wrapped loop. Attach the clasp before wrapping (**photo d**).

❻ For the loop end of the clasp, attach a 4mm bead to the end of the chain as in step 5, but attach 1-2 in. (2.5-5cm) of chain with large links that will accommodate the clasp to the other end of the bead.

❼ To finish, string a small bead on a head pin and begin a wrapped loop above it. Attach this loop to the end of the large-link chain (**photo e**). ◗

– Irina Miech

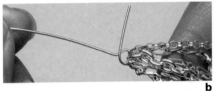

materials

- 66 in. (1.7m) or more Silver scrap chains, different sizes and shapes
- 20 or more Leftover beads, pearls, crystals, stones, etc.
- 4 4mm Sterling silver beads or crystals
- 2 Wide-mouth cones
- 1 Clasp and 1-2 in. (2.5-5cm) chain with large enough links to accept clasp hook
- 1½-2 yd. (1.4-1.8m) 22-gauge Sterling silver wire, half hard
- 1 Head pin

Tools: chain- and roundnose pliers, wire cutter

tip

Safe wire cutting

Here's a simple way to protect your eyes while cutting wire. Hold the wire and wire cutters inside a gallon-sized plastic storage bag. The bag is clear so you can see what you're doing, and it will prevent the cut pieces from flying toward your face. – *Mary Head*

Chain of pearls

These beautiful pearl and chain necklaces support the theory that less is more. If you use high-quality beads in a simple design that doesn't get in the way of the materials, the beads will take center stage, so a little goes a long way.

The simpler of the two necklaces at left is made with five pearls, each sandwiched between silver bead caps. To maintain the classic elegance, the pearl units are strung on wire ending in plain loops and then connected by pieces of drawn cable chain, which features fine, elongated links that draw the eye to the pearls.

The more substantial necklace at far left is made with rollo chain. Because the wide, round links are short, there are more links between pearls. The heavier chain complements the more substantial Bali silver bead caps as do the wrapped loops that complete the exotic look of the piece.

These necklaces can also be made with Czech glass beads instead of pearls and you may omit the bead caps. In this simple, classic design, almost any kind of bead looks good.

Start in the middle of the necklace and make the first pearl unit. Link chain to each loop, attach a pearl unit to the end of each chain, and so on. End the five-pearl necklace with chain and attach the clasp with split rings. End the 12-pearl necklace with pearl units and attach the clasp to them with large wrapped loops.

necklace versions

1 If you will not be making wrapped loops, cut the wire into lengths ¾ in. (2cm) longer than a pearl and 2 bead caps. If you plan to make wrapped loops, cut the wire 2 in. (5cm) longer than a pearl and 2 bead caps.

2 Make a loop at the end of a piece of wire for plain loops or an inch from the end of the wire for wrapped loops, but do not wrap the loop (see "Basics," p. 3 for both kinds of loops).

3 Thread a bead cap on the wire, domed side toward the loop, then a pearl and another bead cap (**photo a**). If your bead caps have very large holes, as in the 12-pearl necklace shown here, string an 8º seed bead between the caps and the loops (**see photo d**).

4 For plain loops, trim the wire to ⅜ in. (1cm) and make the second loop in the same plane as the first. For wrapped loops, begin the second loop in the same plane as the first, leaving a small space for wrapping.

5 Cut two pieces of chain. If you're using drawn cable chain, each piece should have 3 links. If you're using rollo, cut 9-link pieces.

6 For plain loops, open the loops by bending the wire out of the plane sideways (see "Basics") and hook a piece of chain on each loop. For wrapped loops, pull a piece of chain into each loop, then complete the wrap (**photo b**).

7 Make 2 more pearl units and link one to each chain end (**photo c**).

8a. For the five-pearl necklace, repeat steps 5-7 until you have five pearls linked with chain. Divide the remaining desired length of the necklace minus the length of the clasp in half, cut 2 pieces of chain that length, and link them to the end pearls. Attach the clasp parts to the ends of the chain with split rings.

8b. For the 12-pearl necklace, repeat steps 5-7 until the necklace is the desired length, minus the length of the clasp. Then attach the loops of the clasp to the large loops on the end pearl units (**photo d**).

a

b

c

d

earrings

1 String a pearl and a bead cap on a head pin and make a plain or wrapped loop above the bead cap. If the pearl's hole is too narrow for the head pin, enlarge it by drilling it with a broach file. Do not inhale the pearl dust.

2 Open the loop on the earring finding and hook it to the loop above the bead cap.

3 Make the other earring. **o**
– Irina Miech

materials

(16 in. / 41cm necklace)
- **5** or **12-15** Potato freshwater pearls, 6-8mm
- **10** or **24-30** Sterling silver bead caps
- **24-30** Seed beads, size 8º (if bead caps have large holes)
- **10-14 in.** (26-36cm) Sterling silver 6.6mm drawn cable or 2.2mm rollo chain
- **1-4 ft.** (30cm-1.2m) Silver wire, 22-gauge, half hard
- Clasp
- **2** 4.5-5mm Split rings (for 5-pearl version)

optional earrings
- Pair of French hooks
- **2** Bead caps
- **2** Pearls
- **2** Head pins (plain or decorated)

Tools: chain- and roundnose pliers, diagonal wire cutters, broach files if using thicker, decorated head pins

Chain contours

a

b

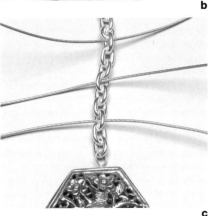

c

d

e

f

g

materials

- **3-4** 16-in. (41cm) Strands of pearls, stone, or glass beads, 6-8mm rounds, or 6 x 8mm rondelles (flattened round beads)
- **2** yd. (1.8m) Flexible beading wire, 0.19
- **6** in. (15cm) 4mm Cable chain
- **3** Focal beads or charms
- **12-18** 2-3mm Beads, sterling silver or gold-filled to match the clasp (optional)
- **1** 3-Strand clasp
- **3** Head pins if using focal beads or **3** split rings if using charms
- **6** Crimp beads

Tools: crimping pliers, diagonal wire cutters, cellophane tape; broach files (optional)

Short lengths of chain give these necklaces shape, versatility, and flair. Dangle special beads or charms from the chain to show off your personal style. You can do so many things with this design—including using the chain to separate groups of same-sized beads of different colors into blocks or showcasing artist glass beads. Use the same concept to create a coordinating bracelet if you wish.

❶ Measure your neckline and subtract the length of the clasp.

❷ Cut the chain into three 2-in. (5cm) lengths.

❸ If using focal beads, follow step 3a; if using charms, follow step 3b.

3a. String each bead onto a head pin. Start a wrapped loop (see "Basics," p. 3) above the bead, and insert the last link of a chain length into the loop before wrapping it (**photo a**).

3b. Attach a charm to the last link of each chain with a split ring.

❹ Cut three 24-in. (61cm) lengths of flexible beading wire.

❺ To center a focal bead or charm on the necklace, start with the piece of chain that has this piece attached. Thread one length of wire through the third link from the pendant bead or charm (**photo b**). Center the wire in the chain.

❻ Thread the second and third lengths of wire through the sixth and ninth chain links respectively and center them. Leave a few extra chain links above the top wire for possible adjustment later (**photo c**).

❼ On the right-hand side of the chain,

string 1⅞-2 in. (4.8-5cm) of beads on the bottom wire. String 1⅝ in. (4.3cm) of beads on the top two wires (**photo d**). Make sure the strands are evenly spaced and the beads are not crowded. Move the wires up or down a link on the chain to adjust for bead size if needed.

8 Repeat step 7 on the wire to the left of the chain.

9 On each side, string the wire through the other chain pieces, passing through the same links as on the middle chain (**photo e**).

10 String an equal number of beads on each side of the top wire until the beaded length is the neckline length you determined in step 1. If you are using pearls or small-holed beads, end each strand with 2-3 spacer beads so the wire will easily pass back through the last few beads.

11 String the same number of beads on each side of the two lower wires. Then

curve the strands into a neckline circle and add enough beads to the bottom and middle wires so the strands form a V-shape at the top of the circle.

12 String a crimp bead on one end of each wire. Then thread each wire through its loop on one side of the clasp. Go back through the crimps and 2-3 beads. Tighten the loops so there is only a small amount of ease around the clasp loops and secure them by taping around the wire close to the beads. Do not cut any excess wire yet.

13 Repeat step 12 on the other side of the clasp (**photo f**).

14 Try on the necklace to check its drape and length. Remove or add beads symmetrically as needed, securing the wire with tape again before checking the fit.

15 When you are satisfied with the fit, crimp the crimp beads on one side of the clasp (see "Basics"). Remove slack along the wires and crimp the crimp

beads on the other side of the clasp.

16 Trim the excess wire on each strand, cutting it flush with the bead it exits. Cut off any extra links of chain at the top of the necklace (**photo g**). ●
– *Pam O'Connor*